QUEST OF LIFE

LIFE TRANSFORMATIONAL JOURNEY

GUNJA GIRI

Made with ♥ on the Notion Press Platform
www.notionpress.com

Contents

Contents

Preface

Life is not a destination; it is a continuous journey, an ever-evolving quest that invites us to discover, learn, and grow. In this journey, we are both the seeker and the creator, constantly shaping the path ahead through our thoughts, beliefs, and actions. Every challenge we face, every triumph we experience, contributes to the unfolding of our unique story.

Quest of Life is a guide through this journey. It is a reflection on the infinite potential within each of us, a call to awaken to the truth of who we are, and an invitation to align our lives with purpose, meaning, and fulfilment. This book does not offer a one-size-fits-all solution, nor does it promise easy answers. Instead, it seeks to inspire you to embark on your own quest, to trust in the process of life, and to embrace the adventure that lies within.

In these pages, you will explore the essential components of a meaningful life –emotional intelligence, spiritual alignment, the power of giving, creativity, mindfulness, and so much more. Each chapter serves as a stepping stone, offering insights and practical tools to help you cultivate personal growth, heal from past wounds, and move forward with courage and clarity.

But more than a guidebook, *Quest of Life* is a reminder that the answers we seek are already within us. This book is not an end, but a beginning, a launching point for your own exploration. The quest of life is ongoing, and it is yours to shape. As you turn these pages, may you find inspiration to live authentically, trust the journey, and recognise the beauty in the unfolding of your life.

For further resources, guidance, and community to support you on your journey, I invite you to visit my website MindoraQuest.com. There, you will find tools, meditations, and ongoing content designed to help you align with your true potential and live a life of purpose and abundance.

Welcome to your quest.

- Gunja Giri

Acknowledgements

The journey of writing Quest of Life has been a deeply personal and transformative experience, and I am filled with immense gratitude for all those who have supported and inspired me along the way.

First and foremost, I would like to express my deepest gratitude to my mentors (my father, Narendra Kumar Giri and my mother Shakuntala Giri), who have guided me on my own quest of self-discovery. Your wisdom, compassion, and insights have shaped the way I view life and have played an integral role in the creation of this book.

I would also like to express my heartfelt gratitude to my family, who have always been by my side on this journey. Rekha Didi and Pooja Didi, your loving prayers and unwavering support give me strength at every step. Your support has been my foundation, and your faith in my vision has fuelled my passion to see this book through to completion. Niraj Bhaiya and Shalini Bhabhi, your understanding and guidance have shaped both my life and this book in a unique way. To my elder nephew Rudransh and younger nephew Ekansh Giri, you both are the joy of my world. Your innocent love and smiles constantly remind me of the true essence of life. This *Quest of Life* would not have been possible without all of you. From the depths of my heart, thank you all.

To my friends and colleagues, I extend my deepest gratitude for your unwavering support throughout this journey. Your patience in listening to my ideas, even when they were still in their raw and unpolished forms, means more to me than words can express. Your constructive feedback, whether through thoughtful critique or encouraging insights, has been instrumental in shaping the clarity and depth of the concepts shared in this book.

You have been a constant source of inspiration, challenging me to think beyond my limits and encouraging me to approach life's complexities with fresh perspectives. Your emotional support has been a comforting anchor during moments of doubt, while your intellectual contributions have enriched the essence of my work.

This book is not just a reflection of my thoughts but also a testament to the collective wisdom, kindness, and brilliance that I have been fortunate enough to find in you. Thank you for being an integral part of this journey.

A special thanks to the participants of MindoraQuest, whose curiosity and commitment to personal growth have inspired me to share the lessons and reflections I have learned throughout my life. Your questions, insights, and willingness to explore the deeper aspects of life have shaped the content of this book and continue to motivate me in my own journey.

I also want to extend my heartfelt gratitude to the incredible team behind *Quest of Life*: the editors, designers, and every individual whose expertise and creativity have played a vital role in bringing this book to life. Your keen attention to detail, professionalism, and unwavering dedication have transformed my vision into a tangible reality, and for that, I am deeply thankful.

A special note of gratitude goes to my first publishing manager, whose guidance, encouragement, and belief in my work have been pivotal in navigating the journey of bringing this book to the world. Your insights and leadership provided the foundation upon which this dream could take flight.

To the entire publishing team, your collective effort has been nothing short of extraordinary. From polishing the narrative to designing the cover, from coordinating timelines to ensuring the highest quality standards, your commitment and hard work shine through every page of this book.

Thank you for being not just collaborators but also believers in the message of *Quest of Life*. This accomplishment is as much yours as it is mine.

Finally, I wish to acknowledge the universe itself, the infinite energy that guides and shapes our journeys. For all the lessons, challenges, and blessings that have come my way, I am eternally grateful. May this book serve as a reminder to all who read it that the quest of life is a continuous unfolding, and that each step is an opportunity for growth, self-discovery, and fulfilment.

With deep gratitude,

Gunja Giri

1

INTRODUCTION

Life is a continuous quest for understanding, growth, and inner peace. The journey involves embracing challenges, mastering the mind, and finding purpose through mindfulness and self-awareness. By cultivating mental clarity and aligning with one's true self, individuals can unlock their potential and live a fulfilled, purposeful life.

The quest of life is the journey each individual undertakes to discover their true purpose, inner peace, and deeper connection with themselves and the world around them. It's a path filled with challenges, lessons, and transformations that shape who we are. At its core, this quest is about gaining mastery over our thoughts, learning to navigate life's ups and downs with wisdom, and ultimately aligning with our authentic self. It's a lifelong journey of self-awareness, growth, and fulfilment – one that leads us to live with meaning, purpose, and joy.

2

WHAT PERSONAL EXPERIENCES HAVE SHAPED MY LIFE JOURNEY? HOW DID I DISCOVER THE QUEST OF MY LIFE?

Let me tell you a short story of my childhood so that you can understand easily.

For a long time, I didn't see my life as a quest. It felt more like a series of situations where I constantly found myself at a crossroads, unsure of which path to take. There were moments when I struggled to make the right decisions, and honestly, I didn't even trust myself enough to choose. Instead, I had developed a habit of listening to what others said, accepting their opinions as my truth, and moving forward based on their guidance. This pattern became a comfortable way of living, but deep down, I knew something wasn't right.

It was in these moments of uncertainty that I began to feel lost. I didn't know how to listen to my own voice or trust my own intuition. There were situations—important ones—where I realised I wasn't making choices for myself. I was just following the flow of others' opinions, allowing them to steer the direction of my life. And each time I did, I felt like I was drifting further from the person I wanted to become.

This constant reliance on external voices made me realise something crucial: no one can truly understand my journey better than I can. My life, my challenges, and my dreams are uniquely mine, and to live a life that truly reflects who I am, I had to stop letting others' opinions dictate my path.

That's when my journey turned into a quest. It became about learning how to listen to myself – my own heart and mind. It wasn't just about choosing between two situations; it was about discovering who I was and what I wanted from life. I had to teach myself that making mistakes was okay as long as those mistakes were mine. And slowly, with each decision I made for myself, I started to trust my inner voice.

This quest of life is not about finding the "right" answers but about learning to make decisions that are true to me, even when the path is uncertain. It's about realising that I have the wisdom within me to navigate my life's journey.

3

A Glimpse Into My Childhood: A World of My Own

When I was about eight years old, I lived in a world of my own, a world I didn't fully understand. It's hard to explain now, but back then, there was a disconnect between me and the reality around me. I wasn't aware of myself or my surroundings in the way other children seemed to be. Self-awareness was something I lacked entirely.

I didn't know much about the people in my life, not even my siblings. I had a brother and sisters, but there wasn't any strong attachment or connection with them. It felt like I was floating in my own bubble, unaware of the bonds that usually tie families together. I preferred playing alone, talking to myself, and creating stories in my mind that no one else could understand. In my own world, I would say all kinds of things while playing, lost in my imagination.

I didn't mind the solitude, but others noticed it. My sisters would sometimes make fun of me, teasing me for being different or distant. They didn't understand, and at the time, neither did I. I wasn't bothered by their teasing, though. This was who I was: someone who lived more in my imagination than in the reality around me.

Looking back, I realise this was the beginning of my journey towards understanding myself. I didn't know it then, but the sense of being disconnected from myself and others was a sign that I needed to embark on a deeper quest, one where I would eventually learn how to become aware of my thoughts, my feelings, and the world around me.

4

My Early Questions and the Beginning of My Spiritual Quest

Even before I became fully aware of myself and my surroundings, there was always a persistent question in the back of my mind: What is this world? I wondered how the universe came into existence, how human beings first arrived, and what it all meant. These questions lingered in my unconscious mind, quietly shaping my thoughts and actions.

I read the Bhagavad Gita and the Ramayana, and after reading them, many of my doubts were cleared. I understood how the universe was created and how humans came into existence, but these explanations were based on a spiritual perspective.

In my family's history, no one had ever gone to a gurukul, and to be honest, I didn't even know that gurukuls existed in today's time. If I had that level of self-awareness back then and could decide based on my consciousness, I might have opted for education in a gurukul.

However, due to family traditions and the norms of that time, I had to go to school. The focus in school education was entirely on science and mathematics, and the scientific theories taught were vastly different from the spiritual concepts I had read. This often left me doubtful, wondering what the truth really was.

During this phase, my spiritual quest became all-consuming. I started believing that if I could just find the answers to the questions that kept swirling in my mind, everything would make sense. I was so deeply involved in this quest that I lost interest in everything else, including daily life. My only focus was finding answers to my spiritual questions.

Around the same time, mobile internet was becoming more accessible, and platforms like YouTube were filled with content on spirituality, history, and meditation. I found myself watching historical series and documentaries, which led me deeper into the realm of meditation. It was then that I learned how meditation could bring one closer to God, and that idea captivated me.

It was during this time that I came across information about the Shri Ram Chandra Mission, where people were taught meditation. Intrigued, I joined and spent some time learning meditation techniques. Meditation became my refuge, a way to connect with something beyond the physical world. However, as life moved forward, my responsibilities increased. College studies, job placements, and career concerns took centre stage, and my practice of meditation gradually faded into the background.

For a while, my spiritual quest took a backseat to the demands of daily life, but the questions never truly left me. They remained, waiting for the right moment to resurface.

5

The Shift from Career to Inner Exploration

After completing my education, I entered the workforce, thinking that a busy professional life would bring the stability and satisfaction I was seeking. But that wasn't the case. I started working in a corporate company as a pharmacovigilance specialist in Chennai, but soon enough, family issues arose, forcing me to leave my job and return home. It felt like everything I had planned was slipping away, and I wasn't sure how to move forward.

Not wanting to remain idle, I decided to start my own business in my hometown. It worked out fine, but despite my efforts and the success of the business, I still felt like something essential was missing. I couldn't quite put my finger on it, but I knew that the fulfilment I was seeking couldn't be found through work alone.

During this period of uncertainty, I turned to meditation again. I noticed that whenever I meditated, I felt a sense of peace that nothing else seemed to provide. I didn't have much formal knowledge about meditation at the time, but the practice itself brought me immense calm. I would often meditate for long periods, simply because it felt right, even though I didn't fully understand the deeper aspects of it yet.

I began to search for more information, spending hours on YouTube and Google, trying to learn whatever I could about meditation. I found several resources online, but most of them required expensive courses or subscriptions, things I couldn't afford at the time. Despite the obstacles, I didn't give up.

That's when I turned to self-help books. They became my guide as I explored not just meditation, but personal growth and mental clarity. I read extensively, absorbing lessons from various authors and thinkers. Slowly but surely, I began to piece together a deeper understanding of myself and the world. The knowledge I was seeking had been within my reach all along – it just took some time and perseverance to find it.

After embarking on my quest for personal transformation, I realised that meditation would play a key role in my journey. Eager to deepen my understanding, I began searching for resources—books, YouTube videos, websites—anything that could provide insight. That's when I came across something truly enlightening: a book that introduced me to the systematic nature of meditation. I discovered that meditation, much like life, has phases, and each phase is carefully structured. This was something I had never considered before.

The book that opened my eyes was based on the Silva Ultramind Method of meditation. José Silva's approach offered a clear, step-by-step process to guide the mind into deeper states of consciousness. The Silva Method provided the exact structure I was looking for, bridging the gap between random meditation practices and a comprehensive, transformational tool. It wasn't just about calming the mind; it was about harnessing the mind's power to make better decisions, improve life, and tap into one's own intuition.

This was a pivotal moment in my journey. It showed me that meditation is not a vague or abstract practice, but a well-organised path with stages, each bringing you closer to your true self.

As I delved deeper into the Silva Ultramind Method, I realised that meditation isn't just about sitting in silence; it's a process, and each phase brings you closer to mastery over your mind and life. I was fascinated to learn that meditation can be broken down into structured phases, which can be followed systematically.

6

How to Follow the Phases of Meditation

1. **Phase 1: Relaxation**
2. **Phase 2: Alpha State (Mind Relaxation)**
3. **Phase 3: Problem-Solving and Visualisation**
4. **Phase 4: Higher Consciousness (Theta State)**

By following these phases, meditation became not just a daily routine for me but a life-changing practice. Each phase brought a new layer of insight and helped me connect more deeply with my own intuition. This systematic approach was exactly what I needed to find peace, clarity, and purpose in my life.

Before I found this book, it felt like something essential was missing from my life. I had everything—a stable life, a routine, and the resources I needed—but there was a sense of emptiness. Life felt mechanical, and the joy I was seeking seemed out of reach. Even with all the external things in place, I wasn't truly living. I wasn't connected to myself in the way I needed to be.

It was as though I was going through the motions, but the deeper meaning—the satisfaction and fulfilment—just wasn't there. That's when I began searching for answers. I explored meditation, watched countless YouTube videos, read articles, and tried different techniques. Yet, none of them gave me the breakthrough I needed.

As I continued to practice the Silva Ultramind Method, I experienced profound changes in my life. Each day brought a new level of depth and understanding in my meditation practice, making it not just a routine but a source of joy and fulfilment. I could feel the positive shifts within me – my mind became clearer, my emotions more balanced, and my intuition sharper.

This transformation ignited a passion in me. I realised that keeping this gift of meditation to myself wouldn't do justice to the journey I had undergone. The happiness and clarity I found were too precious and should be shared with others. I felt a strong calling to contribute to humanity, to help others discover the peace and empowerment that meditation had bestowed upon me.

With this newfound purpose, I decided to dedicate my life to this work. I began to immerse myself completely in the study further. I read numerous books, practiced various techniques, and delved into different meditation methods to expand my understanding. My focus intensified as I sought to refine my skills and knowledge, eager to learn everything I could about guiding others on their journeys.

Many books I read and practices I tried not only enhanced my meditation skills but also equipped me with insights that I could share with others. I became more determined than ever to help people unlock their potential through meditation, by which everyone can quest their life wisely, just as I had done. It was a thrilling realisation that my journey had transformed into a mission, one that would allow me to be a beacon of light for others searching for clarity and purpose in their lives.

There are countless meditation-related books available, covering various techniques, philosophies, and personal experiences.

"Life's meaning is not in discovering oneself, but in creating oneself."

- Rabindranath Tagore

This quote inspires us to realise that the true essence of life lies not in merely recognising who we are, but in actively constructing our radiant identity.

It emphasises the importance of personal growth and self-creation as we navigate our journey.

As I continue to delve deeper into meditation, I realise that **meditation is not just a practice but the method for the quest of life**. If we are to live life fully, it becomes essential to first understand ourselves: who we are, why we are here, and what our purpose is. Life gains true meaning when we embark on this quest to uncover our own essence. Just as Newton's laws were not random discoveries but were rooted in deeper truths of the universe, nothing in this world happens without a reason. Every existence, every discovery, and every thought has its own place and purpose in this vast cosmos.

7

SO, HOW DO YOU ATTAIN THIS STATE OF MIND?

It starts with recognising that your thoughts hold incredible power. By focusing on positive, wealth-oriented thoughts and envisioning your goals with clarity, you align your mindset with the principles of abundance. This involves adopting a perspective that believes in possibilities rather than limitations.

To enter this mindset, practice the following:

1. **Set Clear Goals**: Define what wealth means to you, not just in monetary terms, but in a holistic sense. What do you desire to create in your life?

2. **Visualise Success**: Spend time each day visualising yourself living in that state of abundance. Imagine the feelings, the experiences, and the achievements that come with it.

3. **Cultivate Gratitude**: Develop an attitude of gratitude for what you currently have. This not only shifts your focus from scarcity to abundance but also opens the door for more opportunities.

4. **Take Inspired Action**: While mindset is crucial, don't forget to take action. Listen to your intuition and follow the opportunities that arise, even if they seem unconventional.

As you cultivate this mindset, you will find that the universe begins to respond in ways you never expected. The path to becoming rich is not solely about hard work; it's about aligning your thoughts, beliefs, and actions with the abundance that exists all around you.

The word **"impossible"** has no place in a life driven by intention and possibility. Just as it was removed from the dictionary, you too can eradicate this limiting belief from your life. Success is attracted to those who focus on it, while failure lingers for those who dwell on their setbacks.

One of our common shortcomings is that we often base our perceptions on past experiences, failures, and habits. Our opinions can become rigid, blinding us to the potential for growth and change. As **K. Ford** wisely noted, victory in seemingly impossible and challenging situations often arises from making difficult decisions.

I am the creator of my own destiny and the sovereign of my own mind. This truth holds immense power. We possess the capability to shape our destinies and control our thoughts. It is essential to recognise that we are part of a vast universe – the Earth, the moon, and all living creatures. Everything is interconnected, and all matter is energy, intricately woven into the fabric of the greater cosmic energy.

What we think has the potential to manifest in our lives. Therefore, it is crucial to cultivate a mindset that embraces possibility rather than limitation.

By consciously choosing to focus on positive thoughts, aspirations, and opportunities, we align ourselves with the abundant energy of the universe. This shift in perspective not only empowers us to overcome obstacles but also enables us to create a reality where our dreams become tangible.

The complexity of thoughts shapes the outcomes we experience in life, producing both good and bad results. Yet, there are few individuals in this world who truly recognise the profound impact of their thoughts. Many remain unaware of the significance that thought holds in shaping our realities.

Bhavana, or the power of reasoning and thought, is one of the most precious gifts bestowed upon humanity. Those who have learned to harness this power have achieved everything they have ever desired.

Let's explore this concept from both scientific and spiritual perspectives. From a scientific viewpoint, **Rhonda Byrne's** book, *The Secret*, published in 2006, highlights the transformative power of thoughts. Through engaging narratives, it illustrates that organising your thoughts properly can lead to a more fulfilling life. When we align our thinking with our aspirations, life becomes significantly easier.

However, it's crucial to control your thoughts with discernment, as thoughts themselves lack the ability to differentiate between right and wrong, good and bad. **Byrne** emphasises that focusing on problems will only attract more troubles, while nurturing a positive mindset is essential for overcoming fears.

Our beliefs are the unseen threads woven into the fabric of our lives. They are often deeply rooted in faith, shaped by the religions we follow and the societal norms we embrace. These beliefs become the lenses through which we perceive the world, influencing our thoughts, actions, and ultimately the course of our lives.

At the heart of human existence lie two fundamental forces: Desire (Ichha) and Need. From the innocence of childhood to the maturity of old age, these two forces remain our constant companions. They are the invisible architects of our mental landscape, shaping every thought and decision we make.

8

Understanding Desire and Need

To grasp the profound influence of desire and need, let's consider a simple example. Imagine a child in a toy store. The child's desire might be to own the most colorful and intricate toy on the shelf, a longing fueled by curiosity and attraction. However, the child's need might be as basic as having a toy to play with—any toy that provides joy and entertainment. The interplay between this desire and need sparks a thought: "Should I ask for the expensive toy, or will the simpler one suffice?" This internal dialogue is not limited to childhood; it persists throughout our lives, taking on more complex forms.

As adults, the distinction between desire and need becomes even more critical. For instance, someone might desire a luxurious car, while their actual need might be a reliable vehicle to commute. When desires dominate, they often lead to excessive thoughts, unnecessary stress, and even dissatisfaction. However, when needs are prioritized, thoughts tend to align with practicality and contentment. Recognizing this difference is the first step toward mastering our mental landscape.

9

The Role of Discernment and Conscience

Desire and need generate thoughts, and these thoughts act as seeds planted in the garden of our mind. The direction these thoughts take depends largely on discernment (the ability to judge well) and conscience (the inner sense of right and wrong). Both discernment and conscience are shaped by our environment—the people we interact with, the values we are taught, and the experiences we accumulate.

Let's explore this idea with an example. Imagine a student preparing for an exam. The desire might be to excel and achieve top marks, while the need is to understand the subject thoroughly. Discernment helps the student prioritize studying effectively rather than seeking shortcuts, while conscience reminds them to avoid unethical practices like cheating. The outcome of their efforts—success or failure—is determined by how well they balance these internal forces.

10

The "Take and Give" Rule

The dynamic interplay of thoughts can be understood through the "Take and Give" rule. What we take from our environment—ideas, beliefs, and influences—shapes our thoughts. In turn, what we give back—our actions, words, and decisions—creates our experiences and molds our destiny.

Consider a garden as a metaphor for the mind. If you take good seeds (positive thoughts) and plant them in fertile soil (a supportive environment), you will nurture a thriving garden. However, if you neglect it or allow weeds (negative thoughts) to grow, the garden's potential will be compromised. Similarly, by consciously "taking" positivity from our surroundings and "giving" back constructive actions, we can create a harmonious and fulfilling life.

11

Shaping Destiny Through Thought

Ultimately, our thoughts are the architects of our destiny. By understanding the forces of desire and need, using discernment and conscience as guides, and following the "Take and Give" rule, we can steer our lives toward meaningful and purposeful outcomes.

For example, a person who desires financial success must first identify their true need: Is it security, freedom, or the ability to help others? By aligning their thoughts with this need, they can take steps that are both practical and ethical. Their discernment will help them avoid harmful shortcuts, and their conscience will keep them grounded in their values. Over time, their consistent thoughts and actions will lead them to a destiny shaped by intention and integrity.

In a easy way, life is a delicate balance of desire and need, influenced by our beliefs, shaped by our thoughts, and guided by discernment and conscience. By embracing this balance and understanding the "Take and Give" rule, we can transform our mental landscape and design a destiny that resonates with our true selves.

Thought involves the complex mental processes of reasoning, including judging, reflecting, imagining, and forming ideas or opinions. It is a dynamic and intricate function of the mind, enabling individuals to process information, evaluate experiences, and draw conclusions. These processes are fundamental to decision-making, problem-solving, and creativity, helping humans navigate both their inner world and the world around them effectively.

But this is something we all know and readily available on the internet, accessible to anyone who searches for them. The real question is: **Have you ever considered that thoughts carry charges, just like electricity?**

In the same way that electricity has positive and negative charges, thoughts also possess a polarity, positive and negative. Thoughts have their own intensity so that they become powerful, much like the strength of an electrical current depends on voltage. The more intense the thought, the more powerful it becomes.

But where does this intensity come from? Surprisingly, the source of this intensity is within you. Your emotional states and life experiences act as the fuel for this intensity. Let us explore a few key sources that give thoughts their intensity:

1. Anger

Anger: A Double-Edged Source of Energy

Anger is one of the most powerful emotions a human can experience – a force so potent that it can either build or destroy, depending on how it is channelled. When anger ignites your thoughts, it fuels them with unparalleled intensity and urgency. This intensity, if understood and directed positively, has the potential to spark remarkable transformations.

For instance, history stands as a testament to how anger against injustice has ignited revolutions, brought about social reforms, and empowered individuals to challenge oppressive systems. It is in these moments that anger transcends its destructive nature and becomes a catalyst for profound change.

But here lies the key: the true power of anger depends on your ability to channel it constructively. Anger, if left unchecked, can consume and weaken you, turning into resentment or chaos. However, when anger is transformed into purposeful action, it becomes a driving force that not only challenges the status quo but also creates new possibilities for growth and progress.

In the quest of life, anger serves as a reminder that even the most intense emotions have a purpose. It teaches us that every surge of energy within us, no matter how volatile, can be harnessed to shape our reality. The journey lies in recognising anger not as an enemy but as a tool – a source of energy that, when wielded wisely, can inspire courage, strength, and transformation.

2. Pain

Pain: A Gateway to Profound Realisation

Pain, whether physical or emotional, is one of life's most

potent sources of intensity. It acts as a mirror, reflecting truths we often overlook and compelling us to delve deep within ourselves. Unlike fleeting emotions, pain lingers, sharpening our awareness and forcing us to confront the essence of our experiences. In the depths of pain, we uncover layers of understanding that remain hidden in times of ease and comfort.

Pain, though often seen as a burden, holds within it a profound transformative power. It disrupts the ordinary flow of life, making space for introspection and growth. Many who have walked through the fires of suffering emerge not weakened but strengthened, discovering untapped reservoirs of resilience and wisdom. This transformation is not accidental; it is the result of pain's ability to strip away illusions and bring clarity to our thoughts.

Sometimes, pain becomes a teacher, guiding us to recognise the lessons embedded in hardship. It transforms ordinary thoughts into profound realisations, giving birth to creativity, innovation, and an unyielding strength of character. Far from being an obstacle, pain serves as a force that propels us forward, helping us connect with our deepest potential and reshaping our reality with newfound purpose.

3. Disappointment

Disappointment: A Pathway to Clarity and Renewal
Disappointment stems from unmet expectations, and its initial sting can be disheartening. Yet beneath this

discouragement lies an opportunity, a chance to pause, reflect, and realign. Disappointment acts as a signal, urging us to reassess our aspirations and the paths we've chosen. It compels us to refine our thoughts, sharpen our focus, and develop a clearer, more deliberate approach towards our goals.

When viewed through the lens of growth, disappointment transforms from a roadblock into a powerful source of determination. Redirecting the energy of disappointment allows it to fuel resilience and rekindle the drive to succeed. It is in these moments of recalibration that some of life's most profound breakthroughs occur, as we learn to navigate setbacks with wisdom and grace.

In the quest of life, emotional states like **anger, pain, and disappointment** are not obstacles but unseen forces that amplify the intensity of our thoughts. These forces, when consciously understood and channelled, have the potential to awaken extraordinary power within us. They turn ordinary ideas into transformative actions and pave the way for profound personal evolution.

The key lies in awareness: recognising these emotions not as burdens but as tools that can shape our thoughts and actions with intention. By embracing this perspective, we not only deepen our understanding of the mind's potential but also unlock practical ways to harness it. This approach transforms disappointment into determination, pain into wisdom, and anger into courage, guiding us toward a life of purpose, growth, and fulfilment.

12

The Dual Nature of Thought Intensity

Anger, pain, and disappointment are powerful sources of thought intensity that can manifest as either positive (plus) or negative (minus). The impact of this intensity depends on how you process and channel these emotions.

Positive Intensity

When emotions like anger, pain, or disappointment are constructively harnessed, they fuel determination and drive growth. Positive affirmations, such as "immerse yourself completely," activate inner strength, aligning thoughts with goals and inspiring action. For example, anger can motivate change, pain can build resilience, and disappointment can foster better strategies. Positive intensity turns emotions into powerful catalysts for success.

Negative Intensity

Negative intensity, on the other hand, stems from internalised self-doubt or external criticism. Statements like "you're not capable" weaken thoughts, creating a cycle of self-doubt and fear. This often leads to depression, anxiety, and strained social interactions, trapping individuals in a state of limitation and inaction.

Shifting Intensity

Awareness is key to mastering thought intensity. Positive practices include:

- **Affirmative Self-Talk:** Replace negative thoughts with empowering affirmations.
- **Silencing Negativity:** Reject external criticism and replace it with self-belief.
- **Channelling Emotions:** Transform anger into action, pain into lessons, and disappointment into perseverance.

A Powerful Reminder

The voice you listen to most is your own. Align it with positivity to amplify your thought power. While negative intensity diminishes potential, positive intensity transforms it into growth and success. The choice is yours to make.

13

Transforming Pain into Purpose: The Art of Rising Above Mediocrity

If you find yourself dissatisfied with your current circumstances or the path you are treading, recognise this as a sign from within – a call to evolve into something greater and achieve something beyond the ordinary. Life has designed you for extraordinary possibilities, and dissatisfaction is not a punishment but a nudge, urging you to rise above mediocrity and align with your higher purpose.

In such moments, resist the pull of negative energy that drags you into despair. Instead, actively seek the light within and shift your focus towards positivity. Think of a river carving its path through a rocky terrain – it doesn't stop when met with obstacles. It adapts, redirects, and ultimately finds its way to the vast ocean. Similarly, you have the power to overcome any hurdle and reach unimaginable heights.

Pain, often seen as a weakness, can become your greatest strength if you channel it correctly. It's like the process of refining gold – fire doesn't destroy it; instead, it purifies and enhances its brilliance. Your pain holds the potential to illuminate your path and make your life profoundly meaningful.

Take the example of great innovators and leaders who dared to think differently. Think of Nikola Tesla, whose vision of wireless energy was mocked and misunderstood in his time, yet today forms the foundation of modern technology. Or consider Vincent van Gogh, who painted masterpieces in solitude and struggle, only to have his genius recognised after his death. These individuals endured immense pain but turned it into their power to create something timeless.

Those who dream differently and see the world from a unique lens often face challenges that ordinary minds cannot comprehend. This disconnect can lead to feelings of isolation, often misinterpreted as depression, anxiety, or other psychosocial issues. Society, bound by its comfort in the familiar, tends to suppress what it doesn't understand. People with unconventional ideas are labelled as "ill" or "unstable" and are often subdued with medication, their creativity dimmed before it can shine.

Imagine a child building an unusual contraption out of everyday objects. To the untrained eye, it looks like a mess, but to the child, it's a prototype for something groundbreaking. Instead of encouraging such imagination, society often discourages it, forcing the child to conform. Over time, this suppression leads to frustration and self-doubt, making the individual believe they are flawed.

But the truth is far from it. What you may perceive as a weakness or a struggle could be your greatest gift.

Instead of succumbing to the labels imposed by others, take a moment to realign your thoughts. Think of it as tuning an instrument – by adjusting a few strings, you can produce a melody that resonates with your true essence.

You are not destined to merely follow the footsteps of others; you are here to carve your own path. Your journey may be challenging, but it is uniquely yours. Embrace the power of your pain, let it fuel your growth, and trust in your ability to create something extraordinary. Remember, the most breathtaking flowers often bloom in the harshest conditions. Let your life be a testament to this truth.

14

I DESERVE

"I deserve" is not just a statement; it is a force, an affirmation that vibrates with power and intensity. It is a declaration to the universe, a message that I am ready to claim what is inherently mine. It is not spoken out of arrogance but from the unshakeable truth of my existence: I am worthy.

To say "I deserve" is to ignite the strength within, to awaken the power that often lies dormant. It is not about pleading or waiting for permission. It is about stepping into the fullness of my being and owning my potential unapologetically. The phrase holds immense intensity because it requires belief, courage, and action to wield it.

I deserve love, not the kind that merely comes from others but the unyielding love I give to myself. This love is not conditional; it does not waver. It is the foundation of my strength, a force that allows me to embrace my flaws and celebrate my triumphs.

I deserve success, not because the world owes it to me, but because I am willing to work for it, to endure the challenges, and to rise stronger every time I fall. My thoughts are powerful enough to shape my reality, and by aligning my focus with my desires, I create the life I envision.

I deserve peace, not as a distant goal, but as a birthright. Peace is not given; it is claimed by silencing the noise of doubt and fear and anchoring myself in the present moment.

The power of "I deserve" lies in its ability to transform my mindset. It pushes me to let go of self-limiting beliefs, to stand tall, and to acknowledge that my worth is not defined by external circumstances. When I embrace "I deserve," I stop seeking validation from the world and start trusting the immense power within me.

It is a thought so intense that it reshapes my destiny. By believing in what I deserve, I align myself with opportunities, abundance, and growth. The universe responds to my conviction, and doors open that once seemed locked.

"I deserve" is not just a phrase; it is a promise I make to myself a promise to never settle for less than what I am capable of achieving. It is the battle cry of my soul, the fuel that drives my actions, and the anchor that keeps me focused on my purpose.

To use "I deserve" is to unleash a force so powerful that it transforms not just my life but the world around me. It is the ultimate declaration of self-belief, the foundation of all that I will create and become.

15

The Science of Mind: Understanding the Mind-Body Connection

In the journey for the quest of life, one of the most profound realisations we can have is the deep, intricate connection between the mind and body. The mind is not separate from the body; it is the energy that drives and influences the physical world we experience. The mind and body are continuously interacting, shaping one another in a dynamic way that ultimately determines our health, happiness, and success.

16

The Mind as a Powerful Architect

The mind is the architect of our reality. Everything we perceive—our thoughts, feelings, and beliefs—affects our physical well-being. Neuroscience tells us that our brain has the remarkable ability to rewire itself throughout our lives, a phenomenon known as neuroplasticity. This means that our thoughts have the power to literally reshape our neural pathways, influencing everything from our emotional state to our physical health.

When we think positively, our brain releases neurotransmitters like dopamine and serotonin, which promote feelings of well-being, happiness, and relaxation. These chemical shifts don't just affect our emotional state; they have direct implications for our body's functions, strengthening the immune system, reducing stress, and promoting healing.

Conversely, negative thoughts—rooted in fear, anxiety, or doubt—can have a harmful effect on our health. Chronic stress, for instance, can trigger the release of cortisol, a stress hormone that, when elevated for long periods, can suppress immune function, increase inflammation, and even contribute to the development of chronic diseases.

17

The Body Reflects the Mind

The mind-body connection isn't just a concept; it is a reality that plays out every day in the way we feel, think, and act. Our emotions and beliefs are embodied in the physical world through the way we hold ourselves, our posture, our facial expressions, and even the diseases we develop.

When we are under stress, our body responds by tightening muscles, increasing heart rate, and activating the fight-or-flight response. This is an example of how our thoughts can trigger physical reactions. On the other hand, when we practice relaxation techniques, such as meditation, deep breathing, or positive visualisation, our body begins to respond in ways that promote healing and balance.

Understanding this mind-body relationship is key to unlocking personal transformation. If we can learn to shift our thoughts, beliefs, and emotions, we can profoundly impact our physical health. Meditation, for instance, has been shown to reduce stress, lower blood pressure, and even improve immune function. Similarly, practising gratitude has been linked to better heart health and a more positive outlook on life.

18

THE ROLE OF CONSCIOUSNESS IN HEALING

One of the most powerful aspects of the mind-body connection is the role of consciousness in healing. Our consciousness—the awareness of our thoughts and emotions—holds the key to unlocking the body's healing potential. By cultivating a mindful awareness of our thoughts and emotions, we can begin to identify and release negative patterns that may be hindering our physical and emotional well-being.

In recent years, the field of mind-body medicine has grown exponentially, bringing together science, psychology, and spirituality to explore how consciousness affects health. Practices like mindfulness meditation, yoga, and energy healing have been proven to activate the body's natural healing mechanisms, helping individuals recover from illness, reduce chronic pain, and improve overall well-being.

19

Harnessing the Power of the Mind-Body Connection

To truly harness the power of the mind-body connection, it is important to recognise that we are not passive participants in our health. We have the ability to influence our physical well-being through our thoughts, emotions, and actions. Here are some ways to cultivate this awareness:

1. **Practice Mindfulness:** Mindfulness helps us become aware of our thoughts and emotions, allowing us to observe them without judgment. This awareness creates space for us to choose healthier, more positive thought patterns that support our overall well-being.

2. **Adopt Positive Beliefs:** The beliefs we hold about ourselves and the world around us play a significant role in our health. By consciously adopting beliefs that support our health and happiness, we can change our physical experience.

3. **Engage in Body-Based Practices:** Practices like yoga, which integrate movement, breathwork, and meditation, promote a harmonious balance between mind

and body. These practices help to release stored tension, improve circulation, and increase overall vitality.

4. **Visualise Healing:** Visualisation is a powerful tool for healing. By vividly imagining the body in a state of perfect health, we can direct the mind's energy to support the body's natural healing processes.

5. **Cultivate Gratitude and Compassion:** Positive emotions, such as gratitude and compassion, not only enhance our emotional state but also have a direct impact on our physical health. Research has shown that gratitude can lower blood pressure, improve immune function, and promote a positive outlook on life.

20

The Power of Thought: Creating the Life You Desire

At the heart of the mind-body connection is the idea that our thoughts shape our reality. By consciously directing our thoughts, we can create the life we desire, whether that involves health, wealth, success, or happiness. This is the true power of the mind: the ability to shape our physical world through our mental focus.

By understanding the science behind the mind-body connection, we can begin to consciously design the life we want. It's not just about thinking positive thoughts – it's about embodying those thoughts, aligning our beliefs and actions with our desires, and trusting in the power of our mind to manifest those desires into reality.

The mind and body are not separate entities; they are part of a unified whole, intricately connected and constantly influencing one another. By harnessing the power of this connection, we can live a life of vibrant health, abundant wealth, and limitless possibility.

21

Overcoming Fear and Self-Doubt

Fear and self-doubt can be major barriers in the quest for personal growth. These emotions often stem from deep-seated beliefs that hinder our potential. However, by understanding their origins and applying effective strategies, we can break free from their grip.

22

Breaking Free from Limiting Beliefs

Limiting beliefs are thoughts that restrict our potential, such as fear of failure or feelings of inadequacy. These beliefs are learned and can be unlearned with awareness and action. To overcome them:

- **Identify Negative Thoughts:** Recognise self-limiting thoughts like "I can't do this" or "I'm not enough."
- **Challenge Their Validity:** Ask yourself, "What proof do I have this is true?" Often, there is none.
- **Replace with Positive Affirmations:** Reframe your thinking with empowering statements like "I am capable" or "I deserve success."

By breaking these mental barriers, you open the door to limitless possibilities.

23

THE POWER OF COURAGE AND RESILIENCE

Courage is not the absence of fear but the willingness to act despite it. It is what drives us to take risks and move forward in the face of uncertainty.

- **Embrace Courage:** Recognise that fear is natural, but courage helps you push past it. Each courageous action builds momentum toward your goals.
- **Cultivate Resilience:** Resilience is the ability to bounce back from failure. It's not about avoiding challenges but learning from them and growing stronger. Ask, "What can I learn from this setback?" and use it to propel yourself forward.

Together, courage and resilience help us transcend fear and doubt, leading to personal growth and success.

24

The Spiritual Dimension of the Quest of Life

Connecting with the Universe: Spiritual alignment involves tuning into a higher consciousness and embracing the "universal flow." By doing so, anyone can find guidance in their decisions and navigate life with more peace and clarity. Understanding that we are part of a greater whole connects us to a sense of purpose and fulfilment.

Faith and Trust: Trusting in a higher power—whether it's God, the universe, or a spiritual force—can bring peace and balance to life. Having faith that everything is unfolding as it should allows us to surrender control and trust the journey, cultivating inner peace and strength.

25

THE IMPORTANCE OF SERVICE AND CONTRIBUTION

Fulfilment in Giving: True wealth is not measured by what we receive but by what we give. Contributing to others' well-being—whether through time, resources, or energy—brings a sense of purpose and abundance into our lives. Giving is a means of expanding our capacity for joy and fulfilment.

Law of Reciprocity: The "Law of Circulation" teaches that acts of kindness and generosity return to us in ways we may not expect. By practising compassion and helping others, we contribute to both our own growth and the growth of those around us. This cycle enriches not only the individual but the collective as well.

26

Mastering Time: Creating Balance

Time as an Illusion

Time Management: Effective time management involves more than just completing tasks. It's about prioritising self-care, nurturing relationships, and focusing on growth alongside work. Creating balance means making time for the things that matter most—well-being, reflection, and connection—ensuring a life of fulfilment.

27

BUILDING A LEGACY

Life's Purpose: Identifying your purpose is a foundational step in creating a meaningful life. By aligning your passions with your actions, you can make choices that reflect your true values and contribute to a long-term vision. A clear sense of purpose allows individuals to live authentically and with intent.

Ripple Effect: Even small acts can create lasting impacts. The positive energy we put into the world ripples out, touching others in ways we may never fully understand. Each action, no matter how minor it seems, contributes to the legacy we leave behind, shaping the world for future generations.

28

THE FLOW OF CREATIVITY AND INNOVATION

Cultivating Creativity: Creativity isn't just for artists; it's essential for growth in all areas of life. Innovation often arises when we break routines and approach problems from fresh perspectives. Practices like mindfulness allow for a more open mind, making space for new ideas and solutions.

Embracing Change: Change is inevitable, and embracing it is essential for growth. Fear of the unknown can hold us back, but by adapting to change, we unlock new opportunities for development. Growth lies in our ability to stay open to change and find new ways to approach challenges.

29

THE PRACTICE OF STILLNESS AND SILENCE

Quiet Reflection: Stillness and silence offer a powerful opportunity for self-awareness and deeper connections. Taking time to pause allows us to reflect on our inner thoughts, uncover insights, and reconnect with our true selves.

Clarity in Silence: In the absence of noise, our intuition and inspiration flourish. Silence clears away the distractions of everyday life, allowing for clarity and the space needed to receive guidance and creative ideas.

30

Mindfulness in Daily Life

Living Mindfully: Mindfulness is about being present in every moment, and it can be incorporated into daily routines such as eating, walking, or breathing. These simple practices enhance overall well-being by encouraging us to live with full awareness and intention.

Mindful Decisions: Mindfulness also extends to decision-making. By being present in each moment, we can make choices that are aligned with our true selves. This leads to better decision-making, improved clarity, and greater satisfaction with life.

31

The Art of Letting Go

Surrender Control: Letting go of the need to control every aspect of life opens the door to greater peace. Trusting that life will unfold as it should allows us to release anxiety and embrace the flow of the journey.

Detach from Outcomes: Focusing on the process, rather than fixating on specific outcomes, brings true fulfilment. By surrendering attachment to outcomes, we allow ourselves to enjoy the journey and appreciate the lessons along the way, trusting that each step leads us toward our highest good.

32

THE PURPOSE BEHIND WRITING THIS BOOK

Throughout my life, I've encountered challenges that tested not just my resilience but also my sense of identity. Coming from a financially stable and supportive family, I was fortunate enough to have material comforts. Yet, despite this external security, I often felt deeply unsettled. I was lost, not in the tangible sense, but in a way that gnawed at my soul. Deep inside, I often felt like something was missing. I wasn't truly happy. It felt like I was merely going through the motions, not living a life that resonated with my inner self.

At that time, I didn't have a clear idea of what I wanted to do. There was always this feeling within me, a yearning to do something, to make my mark in the world. But I couldn't pinpoint exactly what that "something" was. Instead of clarity, I felt a growing sense of guilt. Despite being well-educated and having so many opportunities in life, I felt like I wasn't able to achieve anything truly meaningful – something that could make me proud of myself and earn me recognition for my own efforts.

This guilt became a heavy burden. It wasn't just about not meeting my family's expectations; it was also about feeling like I wasn't fulfilling my own potential. I kept asking myself, "What am I doing with my life? Why do I feel so lost despite having everything I need to succeed?"

Looking back now, I realise that this struggle was a turning point in my life. It was the beginning of my quest, a journey to discover not only what I wanted to do but also who I truly am. This discomfort, this restlessness, wasn't a sign of failure; it was a signal from my soul, pushing me to find my path instead of simply walking the one laid out for me by others.

It took courage to admit that I wasn't satisfied with the life I was living. It took even more courage to start questioning everything I had accepted as normal and to begin exploring what truly made me happy. That guilt, which had once felt so suffocating, became a powerful motivator. It pushed me to step out of my comfort zone, to learn, to grow, and to take responsibility for shaping my own destiny.

Then, as if by some cosmic design, life shifted. It was as though destiny itself intervened, forcing me to confront the questions I had long ignored. Who was I? What did I truly want? Why was I here? These questions became impossible to avoid. That was when I embarked on the quest of life: my personal journey of self-discovery and transformation.

In the beginning, I had no idea what this "quest" entailed. The term felt foreign and abstract. At that time, the resources we have today—like advanced social media platforms and accessible self-help techniques—weren't available. I had to carve my path through trial and error, relying solely on my curiosity and determination to uncover answers.

Through persistence, I explored a wide range of books, enrolled in transformative courses, and most importantly, committed to practising the techniques I learned every single day. This daily dedication was the turning point. It became clear that consistent effort, combined with a deep hunger for growth, was the key to unravelling the purpose of my existence.

This journey wasn't just about finding answers; it was about rediscovering joy, energy, and clarity. For the first time, I felt a profound connection with my true self. I realised that life's greatest gift is the ability to align with our authentic purpose, a realisation that inspired me to help others embark on their own journeys of self-discovery.

To extend this support to others, I created MindoraQuest – a platform designed to guide individuals toward a life of meaning, transformation, and empowerment. MindoraQuest is not just a resource; it's a movement to help you reclaim control over your thoughts, align with your inner self, and unlock your true potential. Through carefully crafted meditation techniques, life-transformational practices, and an abundance of wisdom, MindoraQuest serves as your partner in creating a purposeful and fulfilling life.

This book is my way of extending a helping hand to those who feel lost, just as I did. It encapsulates the knowledge, experiences, and insights that changed my life forever. My hope is that these pages will ignite a spark within you, a spark that compels you to take your first step toward discovering who you truly are.

Your journey is yours alone, and within you lies boundless potential. Whether you've just begun to question your purpose or have been searching for answers for years, this book is here to guide you. It is my sincere wish that it becomes the light you need to navigate your unique path.

Now, it's time to take action.

Your life is waiting. The answers you seek are within reach, and the power to transform your destiny lies within you. Don't wait for the perfect moment – this is your moment. Let MindoraQuest and this book be the starting point for a life of clarity, purpose, and abundance.

Step into your quest of life. Claim your destiny. Your transformation begins now.

This journey wasn't easy, but it was necessary. It taught me that true happiness and fulfilment come from living authentically, not from fulfilling others' expectations but from following the call of your own heart. And now, as I reflect on this experience, I see it as the foundation of the quest of life – the journey that has not only transformed me but also inspired me to help others discover their unique paths.

If you, too, feel lost or burdened by the weight of expectations, know that you are not alone. Let my story

serve as a reminder that it's never too late to take charge of your life and create a future that truly reflects who you are. Your quest begins the moment you choose to listen to your inner voice.

Conclusion: The Endless Journey Of The Quest

Life is not a puzzle meant to be solved, nor a destination to be reached – it is a journey to be experienced, an ever-evolving quest that mirrors our growth and transformation. Through moments of joy and sorrow, through clarity and uncertainty, each step shapes the person we are and the one we are destined to become.

This quest of life is both deeply personal and universally shared. It invites us to embrace the infinite potential within us, align our thoughts with our deepest aspirations, and live each day with intention and purpose. Along the way, we discover profound truths about ourselves, find healing for the wounds of our past, and create a future led by courage, resilience, and unwavering love.

As you reach this point in the book, remember that this is not the end of your journey – it is the beginning of a new chapter. The insights you've gained here are tools, seeds of transformation, and guides for the path ahead. Trust that the answers you seek already reside within you. Honour your growth, remain open to the unfolding of life, and move forward with an open heart and a curious mind.

To continue supporting you in this incredible journey of self-discovery and transformation, I warmly invite you to explore **MindoraQuest.com**. This platform is designed to guide you further, offering deeper insights, guided meditations, and transformational tools to help you navigate your unique quest. Whether you seek clarity, peace, or a deeper understanding of your purpose, MindoraQuest is a place to nurture your growth and expand your potential.

Life's quest is eternal, and its beauty lies in the infinite possibilities that unfold with every step you take. You are both the seeker and the creator of this journey, and the power to shape it lies entirely in your hands. Craft your path with intention, embrace the wonder of the unknown, and make every moment extraordinary.

The next step of your quest awaits. Visit **MindoraQuest.com** and step into the life you are meant to live.

The journey is yours, and its endless beauty is waiting to be discovered.

About The Author

My name is Gunja Giri, and I am from Nepal. I have completed Master's degree in Pharmacology (M.Pharma), I manage my family business with unwavering dedication. I see myself as a simple and grounded individual who finds immense joy in the little things that life has offer. While I am naturally shy, I blossom into friendliness and openness once I connect with others.

Writing *Quest of Life* has been more than just an act of putting words on paper; it has been a deeply transformative journey for me. In this book, I share the profound lessons I've learned about the immense power of thoughts, the alignment of energy, and the pursuit of a purposeful life. I am a passionate author and a transformational thinker. Through my own experiences, I have discovered that life is not merely about existing but about uncovering our true essence and embracing the boundless potential within us.

I firmly believe in the extraordinary power of simplicity. Simplicity, to me, is the key to clarity and understanding. This philosophy became the cornerstone of *MindoraQuest*, a platform I founded to help guide others on their own transformational paths. Through MindoraQuest, I aspire to empower individuals to take charge of their lives and unlock the treasures of self-discovery and self-mastery.

When I'm not immersed in my work or writing, I cherish moments spent in the embrace of nature.

Meditating amidst the serene beauty of the natural world allows me to find peace and harmony, reconnecting with the profound interconnectedness of all life. These experiences continually inspire me to reflect and grow.

My hope is that *Quest of Life* resonates with readers on a personal level, inspiring them to embark on their own journeys of transformation. Life is a quest, and through this book, I invite you to explore the limitless possibilities within yourself and create a destiny that truly aligns with your deepest desires.

www.ingramcontent.com/pod-product-compliance
Lightning Source LLC
LaVergne TN
LVHW040911150826
845672LV00007B/1994
* 9 7 9 8 8 9 6 9 9 8 3 0 3 *